诸子百家国风画传

Pictorial Biographies of Great Thinkers

孔子

图/文 郭德福

译 秦悦

画传 上册

CONFUCIUS I

济南出版社

图书在版编目（CIP）数据

孔子画传 / 郭德福著. —— 济南：济南出版社，2014.9（诸子百家国风画传）（2017.4 重印）
ISBN 978-7-5488-1329-3

Ⅰ．①孔… Ⅱ．①郭… Ⅲ．①孔丘（前 551～前 479）－传记－画册 Ⅳ．① B222.2-64

中国版本图书馆 CIP 数据核字 (2014) 第 213385 号

◎上海市重大文艺创作项目由上海文化发展基金会资助
◎上海市文化"走出去"项目由上海市文化"走出去"专项扶持资金赞助

孔子画传

出版发行	济南出版社
总 执 行	上海海派连环画中心
	上海城市动漫出版传媒有限公司
	济南出版有限责任公司（济南出版社）
图书策划	刘 军 刘亚军
出版策划	崔 刚 朱孔宝
出版执行	张承军
责任编辑	张雪丽
特约编辑	刘蓉蓉 孙羽翎 余 阳
装帧设计	舒晓春 焦萍萍

印 刷	济南鲁艺彩印有限公司
开 本	210×285 1/16
印 张	12
字 数	185 千字
版 次	2014 年 9 月第 1 版
印 次	2017 年 4 月第 2 次印刷
标准书号	ISBN 978-7-5488-1329-3
定 价	90.00 元（上下册）

诸子百家国风画传
The Pictorial Biographies of Great Thinkers

编委会
The Great Thinkers Editing Committee

总 顾 问	徐麟
编委会主任	朱咏雷
编委会副主任	陈静溪　高韵斐　王世农　何彧　徐慧玲
编委会委员	汤世芬　丁绍敏　赵钢　梅花　张夏
	张鸿　夏凡　殷涛　王廷文　钱斐
	刘军　崔刚　邵炳军　刘亚军　朱孔宝
	曹奕
学术顾问	傅璇琮
总 策 划	上海市人民政府新闻办公室
联 合 策 划	上海报业集团
	山东省人民政府新闻办公室
	河南省人民政府新闻办公室
总 执 行	上海城市动漫出版传媒有限公司
	上海海派连环画中心
	济南出版有限责任公司（济南出版社）
联 合 执 行	曲阜市人民政府新闻办公室
	邹城市人民政府新闻办公室
	商丘市人民政府新闻办公室
	鹿邑县人民政府新闻办公室
	滕州市人民政府新闻办公室
	广饶县孙子文化旅游区管委会

前言

2014年3月，中国国家主席习近平在联合国教科文组织总部的演讲中指出："中华文明经历了5000多年的历史变迁，但始终一脉相承，积淀着中华民族最深层的精神追求，代表着中华民族独特的精神标识，为中华民族生生不息、发展壮大提供了丰厚滋养。"中华传统文化是涓涓流水，润物无声，滋养了世代中国人的精神家园。在中华传统文化波澜壮阔的历史画卷中，诸子百家文化就是其中浓墨重彩的一页。

充满先贤智慧的诸子百家文化，是集中华传统文化、哲学、艺术于一体的文明宝藏：反对暴力，期盼人与人之间和睦相处、以礼相待，这是儒家思想的"仁"道，平等博爱，止息不义战争，这是墨家思想的"兼爱非攻"；遵循自然、万物和谐，这是道家思想的"道法自然"；论兵却主张"不战而屈人之兵"，这是充满智慧光芒的兵家思想……诸子百家的思想，正包含着人们所努力构造的幸福世界中的重要基石。这是中华民族的财富，也是世界文明的重要组成部分。

近代以来，上海作为中华文明走向世界的一个重要窗口，担当着向世界展示中国文化华彩精粹的重要使命。建设充满活力的国际文化大都市，上海更需要放眼全球、放眼全国，以"海纳百川"的精神打造中华文化精品，推动中华文化走向世界。

这套由国务院新闻办公室支持，上海市政府新闻办公室、河南省政府新闻办公室协力出版的《诸子百家国风画传》丛书，化繁难为轻逸、化艰深为平易，充满了思想美、故事美、人性美、艺术美。它将诸子思想中的妙笔华章与国画家的水墨丹青巧妙结合，书香墨趣将诸子的音容笑貌、神采风骨生动地呈现在读者面前。它向世界打开了中华传统文化之门，同时也为中华文化拓展国际文化交流，进行了新的尝试和创新，提供了新的载体和通道。

诸子百家文化精神正如追逐理性、自由与美的古希腊人文精神一般，是人类共同的文化财富。希望诸位读者从这套书出发，分享故事，体验艺术，感悟哲理，开始一段美轮美奂的中华传统文化探源之旅。

二〇一四年九月

Preface

In March of 2014, President Xi Jinping pointed out in his speech delivered in the headquarters of UNESCO, "Having gone through over 5000 years of vicissitudes, the Chinese civilization has always kept to its original root. Unique in representing China spiritually, it contains some most profound pursuits of the Chinese nation and provides it with abundant nourishment for existence and development." The Chinese traditional culture is just like trickling water irrigating and nurturing the spiritual realm of Chinese people. In the long and splendid picture of Chinese cultural history, the contributions of great thinkers are the most glorious chapter.

The wisdom and philosophies of these great thinkers crystallized culture, philosophy and art in our Chinese civilization: Confucian "Benevolence", Mohist "Universal love", Taoist "modeling itself after Nature" and the military teaching about "the attaining victory in war without fighting" are still holding the stage. These fascinating thoughts constitute the cornerstones of an ideal world Chinese people dream of having. These spiritual assets not only belong to Chinese people but also constitute an integral part of the world civilization.

As an important window in modern times, Shanghai has assumed a mission to demonstrate the brilliance of Chinese culture. To construct a dynamic international cultural metropolis and to promote Chinese culture to the world, Shanghai needs a mind so open to the entire country and entire world and a mind so tolerant as the vast ocean admitting hundreds of rivers.

The Pictorial Biographies of Great Thinkers supported by Information Office of State Council and Information Office of Shanghai Municipality is a close cooperation between Information Office of Shandong Provincial People's Government and Information Office of Henan Provincial People's Government. This series in Chinese painting style simplified the complicated history into simple stories revealing the beauty of human nature and artistic creation. The ink painting presented vividly the personalities of great thinkers, attracting reader to explore their great thoughts and ideas. The pictorial biographies helped open the door of Chinese traditional culture to the world, and this attempt also provided a new carrier and channel for cultural exchange.

The brilliant Chinese culture is fascinating. Like the pursuit for reason, freedom and beauty in ancient Greek humanism, the legacy from these great thinkers is also the cultural assets shared by all the humanities. It is hoped that readers can embark on a journey to explore traditional Chinese culture through reading these books.

September 2014

编者的话

《孔子画传》艺术地描绘了孔子好学求索、以学济世的人生。本书由著名画家郭德福潜心十年研究创作，他数次行走在山东、河南的大地上，循着孔子的足迹，遍寻遗址遗迹，连深藏在洛阳城区菜市场里的『孔子问礼老子处』石碑都几经辗转地找到。这为还原生活中的孔子，准备了翔实科学的史实依据。孔子形象的确立，更是通过对孔子家乡曲阜不同年龄男性的写生和对孔子直系后人形象的综合概括，描绘出更接近真实的孔子形象。在艺术手法方面，作者吸收欧洲群像、肖像历史画的多种表现形式和绘画理念，与传统中国水墨画技法相融合，用水墨淋漓的服饰景物与写实生动的人物面容相衬托，让画面具有一种既真切又虚幻的历史沧桑感。在内容方面，以往读者甚至学者都没有关注到的孔子家庭生活、亲情瞬间、日常细节、四时风俗等，均首度在画中展现。此外，孔子在授徒、讲学、周游列国中的故事，都通过画面灵动再现，让人们以一种更加亲切的方式走进孔子的世界。

（左图为《先师孔子》）

Editor's Words

Confucius by the famous painter Guo Defu highlights Confucius' entire life in seeking knowledge and helping the world with the knowledge he sought. Mr. Guo spent a decade portraying Confucius. He made field trips to Shandong Province and Henan Province to visit historical sites where Confucius is believed to have left his footprints. Mr. Guo even took pains to find out in an outdoor market where the stone stele in memory of Confucius consulting Lao−tse actually stood. To present a faithful portrait of Confucius' image, Mr. Guo interviewed Confucius' direct male descendants of different ages. Mr. Guo's artistic creation combined the skills and concepts of European group portrait with traditional Chinese painting style, and so his ink painting of clothes completed the realistic depiction of Confucius expression. Confucius' life seems so real to the readers. Mr. Guo captured and represented for the first time what usually goes unnoticed: touching moments in Confucius family life, customs and practices at that time. Mr. Guo's vivid and thorough delineation of Confucius' teaching, lecture tours and his visits to different vassal states made Confucius' world very approachable to ordinary readers.

(The picture is Confucius The Saint)

孔子画传
CONFUCIUS

目录
Contents
上册

◎孔子尼山学步图
Toddler Confucius

　　公元前551年9月28日，鲁国"以勇力闻于诸侯"的武士叔梁纥梦想成真，他的妻子颜征在于尼山陬邑昌平乡（今山东曲阜东南）产下一名健康的男婴。夫妻俩大喜过望，遂以尼山为念为孩子取名孔丘（字仲尼）。

孔子的父亲叔梁纥此时被封为陬邑宰，因老年得子，他对孔子宠爱有加，呵护备至。一岁多的小孔丘蹒跚学步，一家人其乐融融。仁爱之心在孔子幼小的心灵中扎根。

◎夫子洞

相传为孔子出生处，又名坤灵洞，位于尼山脚下。尼山，原名尼丘山，因避孔子讳，后人改称尼山。

Shu Lianghe, a warrior in the State of Lu "known for his prowess among nobles", had his dream come true on September 28, 551 BC. His wife Yan Zhengzai gave birth to a healthy boy in a place called Zouyi at the foot of Mount Nishan. They were so thrilled with this unexpected birth of a son that they named the boy Kongqiu (Confucius) after Ni Mountain (an honorary title Zhongni). Confucius' father, Shu Lianghe, was a governor (similar to a sheriff) of Zouyi. Delighted with the blessing of having a male descendent at an advanced age, he adored his little boy and showered all of his love on Kong Qiu. The toddler brought so much happiness and harmony to the family, and benevolence started to take root in his heart.

曾子曰："吾日三省吾身。为人谋而不忠乎？与朋友交而不信乎？传不习乎？"（《论语·学而》）

孔子三岁丧父，母亲颜征在独自承担起养育儿子的重担。孔母带着年幼的孔子迁到曲阜城内阙里居住，靠洗衣、种地为生，生活非常清苦，却不忘教孔子识字读书。孔母勤劳坚毅、善良尚学的优秀品德，对孔子产生了深远的影响。

◎孔母教子图

A loving and strict-teaching mother

Confucius' father died when he was three. His mother Yan Zhengzai shouldered all the responsibility of bringing him up. Mother and Confucius moved into a cottage in the city of Qufu, the capital of the State of Lu, and earned a livelihood by washing and farming. Though living a poor life, Mother never gave up nurturing and educating Confucius under very difficult circumstances. She took loving care not only of his daily life but also his studies. Mother's kind and patient teaching exerted a profound impact upon Confucius.

孔子曰："不知命，无以为君子也；不知礼，无以立也；
不知言，无以知人也。"（《论语·尧曰》）

　　据《孔子世家考》记载，即使在生活最困苦的时候，孔母仍购买礼器给孔子做玩具，鼓励孔子勤奋好学、讲求礼仪，可见孔母的忘我之爱。孔子五六岁时就对祭祀产生了兴趣，经常模仿大人，陈设祭器，练习各种祭拜礼仪。

孔母颜征在购礼器玩具图
Sacrificial vessels as toys

据载孔母颜征在以洗衣种地为生生活清
苦却不忘教育孔子读书习字谋求经济最
困苦之时购买礼器给孔子做童年玩具
鼓励孔子自幼勤奋好学讲究礼仪从中
可见孔母的良苦之爱孔子幼年时就对祭祀
礼乐感兴趣经常横行天足陈设祭器陈习
各种礼仪孔母颜征在是孔子人生第一位老师
全面的培大型石史题画孔子首重尊师
谋划图之路在孔子家多收集刻绘复生动
的史实真传漂亮素材亲归征斯图以记生活中
的孔子以记故里孔母育子之传也

郭德福童并题
时军六十有四

According to *The Family Tree of Confucius*, Mother bought sacrificial vessels for Confucius to play with even when they were struggling for survival. Confucius showed great interest in sacrificial rituals when he was a little child. He often learned how to arrange the vessels and practiced different sacrificial rituals. Mother encouraged Confucius to study hard and advocate traditional rites.

仰之弥高，钻之弥坚。（《论语·子罕》）

　　孔母很重视儿子的品德教育，她在教孔子识字读书之隙常讲孔父叔梁纥的英雄故事。孔父是孔母敬佩的爱国英雄，多次为鲁国立下战功。孔父曾勇率三百甲兵，射杀敌将，护送鲁国大夫臧纥突围，又杀回防邑，击败入侵敌军。这些故事深深地刻在少年孔子的心里。

少年孔子听母亲颜征在讲述孔父叔梁纥纥率鲁国战斗故事图

生義孔父叔梁纥纥主齐军士掌鲁国园园防邑之臑勇率三百
甲兵将鲁国主藏纥实金密围之臑叔梁纥纥杀入重围固守
防邑齐军久攻防邑不下只好退真金直此围意主以童泥失也

郭德福

◎孔母讲述叔梁纥爱国故事图
Father as a hero

Mother attached great importance to the cultivation of virtues. Mother always told him stories about his father who was full of valor and heroic spirit. Confucius' father, Shu Lianghe, was a hero winning many battles for the State of Lu. In one of the battles, Shu Lianghe led several hundreds of soldiers to guard their master's escape and successfully broke through the encirclement.

孔子十五志乐于圆

子曰："吾十有五而志于学，三十而立，四十而不惑，五十而知天命，六十而耳顺，七十而从心所欲，不逾矩。"（《论语·为政》）

　　在母亲的教育下，家境贫寒的孔子一边帮助母亲做事，一边勤奋读书，在少年时就因博学而闻名乡里。

　　孔子在总结自己一生时说，"吾十有五而志于学"，表明孔子在少年时就有了"志于学"的信念。

◎孔子十五志学图
A young man with great ambition

Confucius was well-known for his wide range of knowledge under his mother's careful nurturing and strict teaching. Confucius always helped his mother with her household work while studying diligently. Confucius set his mind on study, and "had a strong belief and determination" to commit himself to becoming a great scholar when he was 15.

子曰："学而时习之，不亦说（yuè）乎？有朋自远方来，不亦乐乎？人不知而不愠，不亦君子乎？"（《论语·学而》）

孔子17岁那年，听说鲁国权臣季孙氏宴请士一级的人物，他想父亲是陬邑宰，自己也应是士中一员，便赶去赴宴。谁知被季孙氏的家臣阳虎拒之门外。阳虎对他说："我们家大人宴请的是士，不是你。"孔子初次尝到人生冷暖。同年，孔母去世。他异常悲痛，千方百计找到父亲的墓地，将父母合葬在曲阜城东防山之阴。

青年孔子赴宴被拒图

史载孔子十七岁的时候，鲁国的一位叫季孙氏宴请士，后人物孔子之父叔梁纥曾是鲁国名士，孔子认为自己也应目是士，所以就贸然前往，却被阳虎拒之门外，孔子初次尝到人生冷暖，更加立志当斯图以画记史。一壬辰州

Confucius went to a big party held by a high-ranking official. The 17-year old Confucius naively believed that his father had been a governor, and so he was also a member of officialdom. But quite unexpectedly, he was denied the entrance. "We are entertaining nobles, not you" was the insult shouted at him. Confucius had his first exposure to the fickleness of the world. Confucius lost his mother that year, which made him so sad. He tried to find his father's tomb and buried his father and mother together.

子贡问曰："孔文子何以谓之'文'也？"子曰："敏而好学，不耻下问，是以谓之'文'也。"（《论语·公冶长》）

青年孔子十分好学，经常向有学问的人请教，与之切磋。有人嘲笑他："谁说陬邑宰的儿子懂礼？什么事都问别人。"孔子听到后说："不懂就问，这就是礼啊。"孔子第一次在太庙看到欹器，问守庙人得知，此物无水时倾斜，盛的水适中就立正，盛的水过满就倾覆，是放在君王右座的警示之器，叫右座之器。孔子从中悟出了"满招损，谦受益"的道理。

Young Confucius was very curious and eager to learn, and was never ashamed to seek answers. He would ask "hows" and "whys" about whatever he did not understand. He asked so many questions that he was considered impolite, "The governor's son is so annoying. He seems to understand nothing." When Confucius learned that, he dismissed them, saying, "It is a sign of politeness that you ask about something you don't understand." Confucius wondered about Qi vessel when he saw for the first time in Tai Temple. The janitor explained it to him: the vessel slants when it is empty, but stands upright when it is full of water, and it tips if it is overfilled. Qi vessel usually sits on the right side of the duke as a constant reminder, and is called right-side vessel. From this, Confucius grasped the principle of "Haughtiness ruins and humility benefits".

青年孔子阅欹器图

史载青年孔子
十分好学，经常
向有学问的人请
教，即使进有人
嘲笑，孔子照说
陶邑大夫的儿子
懂礼他什么都向
别人孔子听到说
不懂就问道，这就是
礼啊，青年孔子到
鲁太庙中看到
欹器陶字属人处知
此器名叫欹器
甚为迂中则满
其器一道满就
覆恩放置君主座
的警示之器听听不季
之器孔子听后以
为斯闻以省思考
苟聪道理金将激荡

◎青年孔子问欹器图

An inquisitive Confucius

15

孔子19岁时，迎娶宋国人亓官氏为妻。20岁那年，孔子的儿子诞生。鲁昭公赐了一条鲤鱼作为贺礼，孔子于是给儿子取名为鲤（字伯鱼）。幼年丧父的孔子非常珍惜与儿子相处的温馨时光。冬天雪后，孔子全家在院子里快乐地堆起雪人。

子曰："弟子入则孝，出则悌，谨而信，泛爱众，而亲仁。行有余力，则以学文。"（《论语·学而》）

Confucius married a lady surnamed Qiguan from the State of Song when he was 19. His wife gave birth to a son when he was 20. Duke Zhao of Lu bestowed a carp to express his congratulations and best wishes for the new-born baby. And so his son was named Li (a carp) and his honorary title was Boyu (also a fish). Confucius lost his father at a tender age and he really cherished the time spent with his son. Building a snowman with his son in winter was one of the happy things he enjoyed doing with his family.

◎孔子、亓官氏、孔鲤戏雪图
A happy family playing with snow

孔子27岁时向鲁国著名琴师师襄子学琴。半个月之后，师襄子劝他学习新曲。孔子说："我还没有学到这支曲子的神韵。"又过了半个月，孔子还是没有学习新曲。直到有一天，孔子在琴声中感悟到："除了周文王，谁能作此曲呀！"师襄子深感震惊：这曲名叫《文王操》，正是周文王所作。

子在齐闻韶，三月不知肉味，曰："不图为乐之至于斯也。"（《论语·述而》）

Confucius took Qin lessons when he was 27 from a Qin master Shi Xiangzi of Lu. Seeing Confucius practiced a tune for two months, Xiangzi encouraged him to take a new piece. Confucius said that he hadn't acquired the charm yet. Another two weeks passed, Confucius was still practicing it. Until one day, Confucius came to a sudden realization, "Nobody can compose such a score but King Wen of Zhou Dynasty." Xiangzi marveled at his brightness: The tune is just entitled *King Wen's Virtue*, and it is exactly composed by King Wen himself.

◎青年孔子悟乐图
Comprehending the music by King Wen

守岁，中国民间除夕习俗，从年夜饭开始，一夜不睡，以迎候新年的到来。守岁的习俗，既对如水逝去的岁月含惜别留恋之情，又对新年寄以美好希望之意。

4000多年前中国已有春节（俗称过年），鲁国亦有春祭习俗。孔子和家人一起过春节，燃灯守岁，给儿女们讲傩戏中有关春节的故事。儿子孔鲤做着鬼脸吓唬妹妹，胳膊上挂着迎春傩戏的面具。

◎孔子阖家守岁讲古迎春图
Celebrating the New Year

The custom of celebrating the Spring Festival can be traced back to more than 4000 years ago. It was also an occasion for the spring sacrificial rituals in Lu. Confucius was telling his children festival stories performed in Nuo Opera. His son Kong Li made faces to his younger sister with a Nuo mask on his arm.

古人迎春时，有燃竹子，以其爆裂之声祛除病邪　　燃放爆竹，期盼新的春天带给他们更美好的生活。
的风俗，俗称"爆竹"。孔子与妻子、儿子、女儿阖家

It was a custom in ancient China to burn bamboos in the hope that the cracking sound would drive away illness and evils. Confucius and his family set fire crackers in the hope that a new spring would bring them a better life.

◎孔子阖家爆竹迎春图
Welcoming the spring

子曰："三人行，必有我师焉：择其善者而从之，其不善者而改之。"（《论语·述而》）

　　孔子30岁时办了一件大事——创办私学，成为中国创办平民教育的第一人。西周时期，"学在官府"，教育被贵族垄断。孔子打破了这种局面，提出"有教无类"的办学方针，不分贫富贵贱，不论老少，只要想学习，都可成为他的学生。在孔子所收的学生中，有比孔子小30岁的颜回和只比孔子小6岁的颜回的父亲颜路，有蓬蒿编门、破瓮当窗的原宪，有远道而来的卜商。

◎孔子有教无类办学图
Teaching without discrimination

Confucius was the first person to educate the populace. He set up a private school when he was 30. Schooling was monopolized by government in Western Zhou Dynasty, and it was only the aristocracy's privilege. Confucius advocated the principle of "teaching without discrimination". Whoever wanted to learn, young or old, regardless of his social status and richness, could be his disciples. Confucius had disciples as young as Yan Hui who was thirty years younger than Confucius, and as old as Yan Hui's father Yan Lu who was only six years younger than Confucius, as poor as Yuan Xian whose cottage had straw as door and broken jar as window, and Bu Shang who came from another state.

孔子向学生传授"六艺"：礼、乐、射、御、书、数。其中的"御"就是驾车的技术。孔子的很多学生学会了驾车，其中子路、冉求是驾车高手。在传授驾车技术时，孔子一直倡导安全驾车。孔子说："上车后，要挽住车中绳索，心无旁骛，不能乱说话，不能指指画画。"

孔子倡导安全驾车图

Confucius taught his disciples "six arts": rite, music, archery, driving, writing and math. Many of Confucius disciples knew how to drive carriages, and Zilu and Ran Qiu were masters. When teaching them to drive, Confucius always advocated driving safety. He said, "Hold the reins tightly when you are on board and focus on driving."

孔子驾车技术精湛。达巷街上曾有人说，孔子真厉害，什么都会，只可惜没有什么成名的专长。孔子听说后笑道："那我专练什么呢？驾车？射箭？就让我练驾车好了。"孔子解释道："善于驾驭马匹的人，要会平均使用马的力量，无论回旋还是转弯，都要顺着马的意愿，这样就可以驭马远驰。"善于驭马的孔子经常驾车出行，迎风奋进。

子曰："由！诲女知之乎！知之为知之，不知为不知，是知也。"（《论语·为政》）

Confucius was very good at harnessing a cart. But there was always someone questioning his being good at all skills but expert at nothing. Confucius laughed, "Let me show you something. Driving? Archery? Let me do driving." Confucius explained, "If you want to harness a horse, you should use the forces of horses in a balanced way. You should bend to the horse's will when making a turn or circling around. Only in this way, can you drive horses far." Confucius enjoyed driving the carriage against the wind and advancing bravely.

◎孔子驾车奋进图
Driving carriage

子曰："君子矜而不争，群而不党。"（《论语·卫灵公》）

孔子爱好体育，他教授学生的"六艺"中就有两种体育项目——驾车和射箭。"孔子射于矍相之圃，盖观者如堵墙"，说的就是曲阜人聚集于矍相园林争观孔子射箭比赛的场面。赛后，孔子感慨地说："君子没什么可争的事情，如果有所争，那一定是比射箭吧！赛前相互揖礼走上赛场，赛后痛快地喝酒，那可真是君子的竞赛啊！"

◎孔子师生射箭比赛图
An archery competition

Confucius loved sports. Driving and archery were two sports games in the "six arts" he taught his disciples. Locals in Qufu liked to gather in a garden to watch their competition. Confucius said, " Gentlemen compete for nothing. If they are for something, it must be archery. Bow to each other before the game, and drink afterwards to your heart's content. It is really a gentleman's game!"

孔子常带学生颜回散步。孔子快走，颜回也快走；孔子慢走，颜回也慢走。其实，这是孔子在向身体不够强壮的学生颜回传授快慢相间的徒步健身方法。颜回在学业上，也处处以孔子为榜样，一心一意追随老师的脚步，故称"孔步颜趋"。

Confucius often took Yan Hui for a walk. Confucius walked fast, Yan Hui followed fast; Confucius walked slowly, Yan Hui followed slowly. As a matter of fact, Confucius was demonstrating to Yan Hui, who was not so solidly built, how to improve his health by alternating fast pace and slow pace in their walk. In his study, Yan Hui also followed Confucius steps, modeling Confucius in every way.

◎孔子颜回徒步图
Going for a walk with Yan Hui

孔子身材高大，喜爱体育，也喜欢举重。孔子"力抬城关"，说的就是孔子用双臂举起粗大的"城关"（关城门的门闩），颇有其父叔梁纥的遗风。孔父叔梁纥生前在一次激战中，曾经为了掩护鲁军突围，双臂举起正在落下的城闸，遂以"勇力闻于诸侯"。

子曰："知（zhì）者不惑，仁者不忧，勇者不惧。"（《论语·子罕》）

Confucius was tall and had the same unusual strength as his father. His father Shu Lianghe once lifted a descending city gate in a fierce battle to help the Lu army to break out the encirclement, and was well known for his "prowess among nobles". Confucius himself also lifted a heavy latch that fastened the city gate.

◎孔子力抬城关图
Lifting the latch

孔子力抬城关图

史载孔子身材高大喜爱体育也喜欢举重孔子能
力抬城关孔子甲父叔肹能举起甲关其城门的题大
城关即颜其父叔渫纪的遗风孔又叔渫纪生新鲁国
捧护鲁军突围双臂力举萦万的城关开持记之金和

子曰："知（zhì）者乐水，仁者乐山。知者动，仁者静。知者乐，仁者寿。"（《论语·雍也》）

　　孔子说："聪明人乐于水，仁人乐于山。聪明人好动，仁人好静。聪明人快乐，仁人长寿。"他教育学生乐山乐水，做有道德修养的人，认为一个人应当热爱自然、敬畏自然、融入自然。孔子是最早把生态道德教育融入人伦道德教育的人之一。

◎孔子乐山乐水图
The nature-loving Confucius

Confucius said, "The wise take delight in water; the virtuous in mountains. The wise like to travel and the virtuous prefer serenity. The wise gain happiness and the virtuous, long life span." He taught his disciples to love the mountain and water, and be a cultured person. He thought that a man should love nature, respect nature with awe, and live in harmony with nature. Confucius is one of the first educators who integrated ecological protection into ethical education.

孔子经常带领学生登有"环鲁之山多矣，论其玲珑秀峙，未有此山之奇者"之称的东山（今山东邹城东南的峄山）。孔子带领学生攀岩而上，登顶远望，让学生开阔视野、锻炼毅力、强健体魄，从而留下了"登东山而小鲁"的名句。

◎孔子师生登东山小鲁图
Climbing Dongshan Mountain with disciples

Confucius often took his disciples to climb Dongshan Mountain, a mountain famous for its grotesque rocks (Today's Yishan Mountain, which is located in the southeast of Zoucheng in Shandong Province). Climbing built their willpower and body, and looking down from the peak of the mountain gave them a broader view. The experience of climbing left with us the famous saying "Climbing Dongshan Mountain makes the State of Lu appear smaller".

一次，孔子师生从曲阜出发去登泰山。泰山高而险，　　望远，感慨万千，留下了"登泰山而小天下"的名句。
师生相互携助，终于登上了泰山顶峰。孔子师生登高

◎孔子师生登泰山小天下图
Climbing Mount Tai with disciples

Confucius and his disciples went to climb the high and steep Mount Tai. They helped each other all the way to the top. Confucius and his disciples ascended to the height and had a spectacular view, left with us the famous saying "On the top of Mount Tai, the world seems smaller".

子曰："学而不思则罔，思而不学则殆。"（《论语·为政》）

孔子常泛舟于泗水。望着滔滔而去的河水，孔子感慨过去的人和事以及生命与时间，无不如同昼夜不停的江水一样快速流逝，从而留下"逝者如斯夫，不舍昼夜"的思索和感悟。孔子对水的透彻观察与体悟，影响着数千年的中国文化。

◎孔子泛舟图
Boating on Sishui River

Confucius often went boating on Sishui River. Looking at the current of Sishui, Confucius lamented the bygones: people, things, life and time, and they are all like the flowing water of Sishui, passing by day and night. Confucius thus made the comment: "Time flies on and on for days and nights, just like the flowing water, never stopping." Confucius' observation about water has a profound influence upon Chinese culture.

子曰："默而识（zhì）之，学而不厌，诲人不倦，何有于我哉？"（《论语·述而》）

　　一个晴朗的日子里，孔子与学生子路登山游览。在青山绿水间，几只山鸡在山梁上悠闲嬉戏。它们或啄羽梳理，或互相张望。孔子和子路被眼前和谐美丽的场景所吸引，驻足不前。山鸡见有人来，扑腾飞起，略作盘旋，又落回原地，继续觅食嬉戏。孔子感叹："这些山鸡呀，也懂得时宜呀。发现这里没有人想害它们，就继续留下来。"子路似有所悟，朝着山鸡友好地拱拱手。山鸡望望他们，展翅飞向远方，隐于山雾之中。

◎孔子子路观山鸡图

Pheasants in the mountain

Confucius and his disciple Zilu went hiking on a sunny day in a mountain. There were some pheasants there. They were either preening themselves or walking leisurely. Confucius and Zilu were attracted to this beautiful scene. When seeing some people coming, the pheasants flew up and hovered for a while, and then landed down to continue their food-searching.

Confucius said, "These pheasants are very smart. When they find that we have no intention to hurt them, they just continue what they are doing." Zilu seemed to comprehend something, and he bowed to the pheasants. The pheasants looked back and flew away into the depth of mountain.

子游曰："丧致乎哀而止。"（《论语·子张》）

　　孔子的一位友人原壤因母亲突然去世而深受打击，不能料理母亲的葬礼。孔子慨然挑起帮助友人葬母的担子。孔子亲自挑选棺木，用水调色为棺木上色，描绘图案。原壤在这时本该"致乎哀"，却说自己很久没有唱歌了，随即登上母亲的棺木高歌一曲。邻居见状，纷纷劝孔子别再帮助原壤了。孔子说："谁叫他是我的老朋友呢？我们看在他死去的母亲面上，把葬礼办了吧。"

◎孔子为友人之母"浴椁"图
Painting the coffin for a friend's mother

Confucius' friend Yuan Rang felt so grief-stricken over his mother's sudden death that he was unable to conduct his mother's funeral service. Confucius offered to help. Confucius picked and painted the wood coffin. Yuan Rang was supposed to be in mourning, but he stood on his mother's coffin singing aloud instead, saying he hadn't sung for a long time. Seeing this, Yuan Rang's neighbors all thought Confucius shouldn't handle the funeral. However, Confucius said, "Isn't he my friend? Let me do this just for the sake of his mother."

老子，姓李名耳，字伯阳，又称老聃，春秋时期思想家，著有《道德经》，道家学派创始人。

34岁的孔子一直想问学老子。无奈老子居住的周朝国都洛邑距鲁国太远，清贫的孔子没有旅费前往。孔子学生南宫敬叔向鲁昭公表达了孔子的意愿，鲁昭公决定派一辆车、两匹马、一名随从，助孔子问学老子。

路上，好学的孔子说："吾闻老聃（即老子）博古通今，通礼乐之原，名道德之归，则吾师也，今将往矣。"路经黄河时，孔子射下一只大雁，预备送给老子做见面礼。老子闻讯，亲自出城相迎。

◎孔子见老子图
Meeting Lao-tse

The 34-year old Confucius had always been thinking of learning from Lao-tse (philosopher in the Spring and Autumn Period, founder of Philosophical Taoism). Lao-tse lived in the capital city of Zhou Dynasty. Unfortunately, Confucius had not enough money to cover the trip. One of Confucius' disciples made Confucius' wish known to Duke Zhao of Lu, and the latter sponsored Confucius a two-horse drawing carriage, and one attendant. Confucius thought on his way, "Lao-tse is erudite and informed about the past and present, and he could be my mentor." Confucius presented Lao-tse a wild goose he shot down when passing by the Yellow River. Lao-tse met Confucius at the city entrance.

老子当时任周守藏室之史，职位相当于国家图书档案馆馆长。他对孔子的来访做了认真的安排：先阅览典籍，然后谈礼仪。孔子阅读了《商颂》《周颂》及上古文献三千余篇，为以后编撰《尚书》准备了史料；孔子还重点研读了《周礼》和百余诸侯国的旧志，为后来编撰《春秋》打下了基础。

◎孔子老子阅典图
Two great minds browsing the classics

Lao-tse was then the director of National Library and Archives. He arranged Confucius' visit thoughtfully: Confucius would browse classics first and then they two would have discussions about rites. Confucius read *Ode to Shang Dynasty*, *Ode to Zhou Dynasty* and more than three thousand other articles about ancient times. These readings prepared Confucius for the writing of *Book of History*. Confucius also perused *Rites of Zhou* and many other archives about different states. These readings well prepared Confucius for his writing of *The Spring and Autumn Annals*.

子曰："周监于二代，郁郁乎文哉！吾从周。"（《论语·八佾》）

老子又引领孔子参观周都明堂、太庙和天子郊祭天、社祭地的场所，"观先王之遗制，考礼乐之所极"。明堂是周天子祭祖、朝会的地方，那里有周武王灭商后迁来的九鼎，还有周公的画像。周公是孔子心目中的圣人，因此他在其画像前长时间驻足，后来还多次梦见了周公。

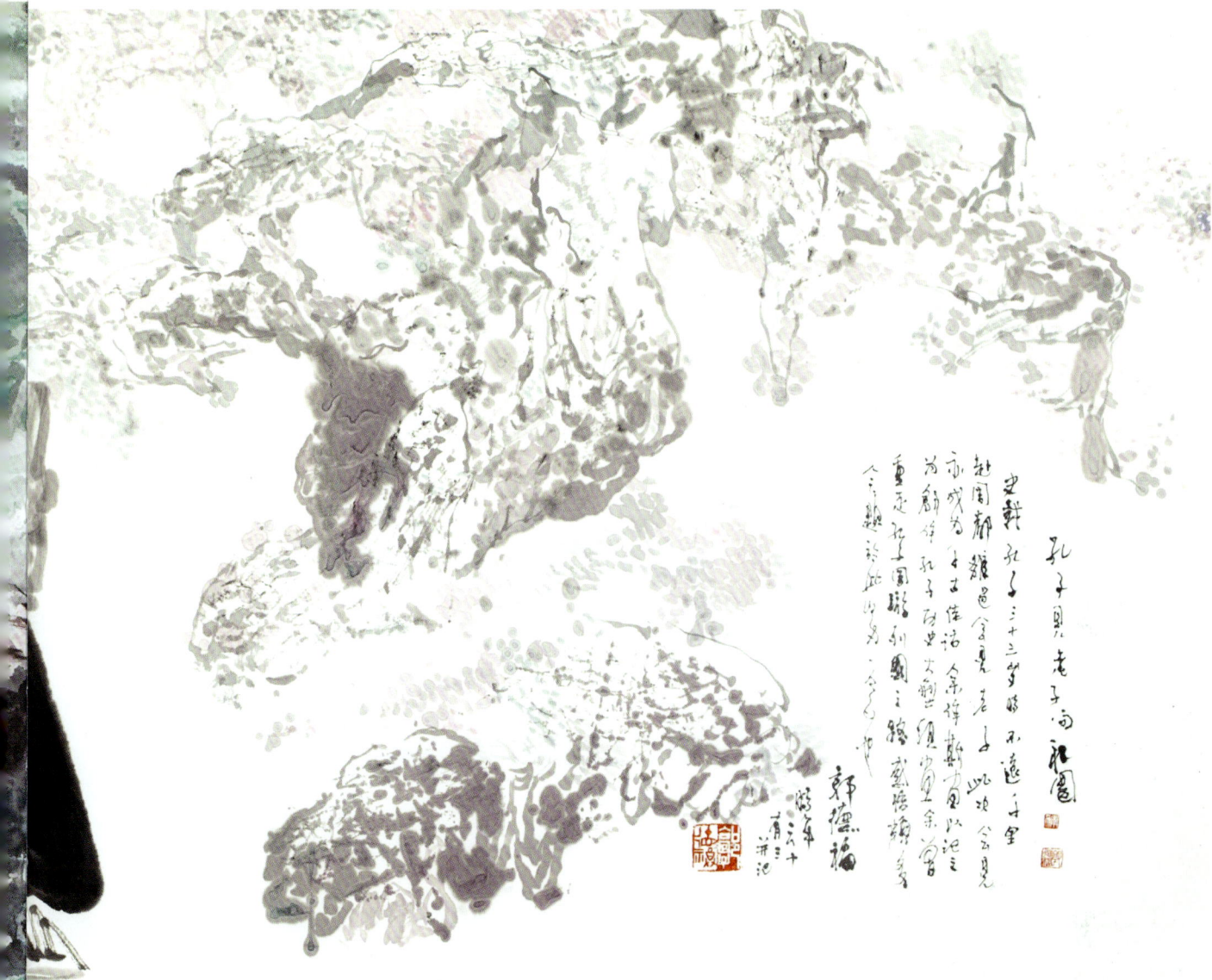

◎孔子见老子问礼图

Touring the worship palaces

Lao-tse showed Confucius around to admire the ritual system passed down and study the practice at its perfection. They toured Ming Temple of Zhou, the Imperial Ancestry Temple, and other worship places, such as place for heaven worship on winter solstice, and place for earth worship on summer solstice. Ming Temple was where the emperor of Zhou paid tribute to his ancestor and held morning meetings. Confucius admired the nine Dings (an ancient cooking vessel with two loop handles and three or four legs; it is a symbol of dynasty) that King Wu of Zhou transported here after he conquered Shang Dynasty. Duke Zhou was a wise man in Confucius' mind, so he stood still before Duke Zhou's portrait for a long time, and dreamed about him quite a few times afterwards.

友直，友谅，友多闻，益矣。（《论语·季氏》）

　　孔子的周都问礼之行，历时近一年。这是孔子一生中最快乐的时光，他几乎每天都有新发现和新思考，并与老子建立了深厚的友谊。分别时，老子深情地对孔子说："我听说富贵之人用财物来送人，仁义之人用言语来送人。我不富贵，只好盗用仁人的名义，用言语来送你。"孔子认真地听完老子的临别赠言，望着老子远去的背影，久久不愿离去。

◎老子寄语孔子图
Lao-tse's advice for Confucius

Confucius stayed and studied in the capital city of Zhou for about a year and developed a profound friendship with Lao-tse. This is the happiest time in Confucius' life. He could have new thoughts almost everyday. When parting, Lao-tse said with emotion to Confucius, "I'm not rich. But let me a benevolent person and offer you some advice." Confucius listened with respect to his parting words, and was reluctant to go.

曾子曰："君子以文会友，以友辅仁。"（《论语·颜渊》）

孔子告别老子，返回鲁国。途中，他的学生问："您觉得老子是个什么样的人呢？"孔子说："天上的鸟会飞，地上的兽会跑，水中的鱼会游。这些，我都知道。只有龙，我无法知晓。它能云里来，风里去，变化莫测，无人能识其全貌。这次见到老子，远远超出我的想象。我想，老子大概就像龙一样吧。"

◎孔子悟龙图
Confucius' understanding of the dragon

Confucius said goodbye to Lao-tse. On his way back to Lu, his disciples asked him, " What do you think of Lao-tse?" Confucius answered, "The birds in the sky can fly, the animals on the earth can run, and the fish in the water can swim. And I understand them all. Only the dragon in legend, I can hardly get hold of it. It can ride on the clouds and disappear in the wind as it wishes. It is so fickle that we cannot know what it is really like. My meeting with Lao-tse is so much beyond my expectation. To me, Lao-tse is as mysterious as the dragon. I can hardly figure him out."

项橐（tuó），春秋时期的神童，孔子曾向其请教过问题，后世尊其为"圣公"。

　　"昔仲尼，师项橐"是《三字经》里的一句话，说的是孔子出行路过中牟时，被一群玩筑城游戏的小孩挡住了去路。孔子下车，微笑着请孩子让路。小顽童项橐理直气壮地说："只有车绕城而走，哪有城让车而行呢？"孔子望着天真的项橐，觉得小孩说得有理，于是说："中牟人可教化。连孩子都如此，何况大人呢？"孔子师从天真，依"理"而动，于是回车绕道而行。

◎孔子回车图

Giving way to kids

Some kids were playing the game of "building a city" and blocked the road. Confucius got off and asked them to make way for the carriage. A kid named Xiang Tuo said, "A carriage should make way for a city, how can a city give in for a carriage?" Confucius looked at the naive kid, nodding with approval, "People here can be educated. Even kids are so reasonable, let alone adults." Confucius did as what Xiang Tuo told and took a detour to avoid the so-called city.

子曰：“苟志于仁矣，无恶也。”（《论语·里仁》）

　　从周都返回鲁国后，孔子门下的学生比以前更多了。一次，孔子与子路、颜回出行，途中闲话时，孔子要他们谈谈志向。子路说："愿意把车马、皮衣拿出来与朋友共同使用，用坏了也不后悔。"颜回说："愿意有功也不夸耀功，有劳也不表白劳。"子路也请老师谈谈志向，孔子说："老者安之，朋友信之，少者怀之（意为"安养老人，成全朋友，关怀少年"）。"

◎孔子"老者安之，朋友信之，少者怀之"图
The aspirations of Confucius

Confucius got more disciples after he came back from the capital city of Zhou Dynasty. One day, Confucius asked Yan Hui and Zilu about their aspirations. Zilu said, "I will share my carriage and fur coat with my friends and will not regret for doing it." Yan Hui said, "I will not boast of my achievements even if I make some; I will not moan my hardship even if I endure it." Zilu asked for Confucius' aspiration. Confucius said, "I would like to give comfort to the aged, trust to my friends and enlightenment to the young."

子曰："饭疏食，饮水，曲肱而枕之，乐亦在其中矣。不义而富且贵，于我如浮云。"（《论语·述而》）

孔子教育学生，只有通过艰苦学习，才能得到知识。孔子最欣赏学生颜回，他说："贤哉，回也！一箪食，一瓢饮，在陋巷。人不堪其忧，回也不改其乐。"颜回少年家贫，是孔子年龄最小的学生之一，却勤奋好学，经过苦读终有所成。

Confucius believed that true knowledge could only be acquired by hard work. Yan Hui was one of Confucius' favorite disciples. Confucius thought highly of him, "How virtuous Yan Hui is! A basketful of coarse rice, a gourdful of water was enough to make him enjoy the poor life in a shabby lane, while other people will find it unendurable." Though Yan Hui was one of the youngest disciples, he studied really hard and made great achieve after hard learning.

◎ 孔子赞颜回图

Confucius praising Yan Hui

孔子闻韶图

Enjoying *Shao* music

◎孔府

位于曲阜城内孔庙旁，是孔子嫡长子孙的府第。

孔子 35 岁那年，鲁国季孙氏、叔孙氏、孟孙氏三大家族发动政变，鲁昭公被迫流亡国外。孔子愤而离开鲁国，去了齐国。孔子在临淄（齐国故都）听了韶乐后，大为惊叹。于是他认真地学习奏唱，一连三个月不知肉的味道。韶乐是虞舜时期的乐曲，也称"箫韶"，因有九章，故又称"九韶"。孔子评论其"尽美矣，又尽善也"，"箫韶者，舜之遗音也。湿润以和，似南风之至"。齐人称赞孔子的学习态度达到了痴迷的境地。

When Confucius was 35, three powerful clans in the State of Lu launched a coup. Duke Zhao of Lu was forced into exile. Confucius also left the country for the State of Qi. Confucius marveled at the *Shao* music played in Qi. He engrossed himself in the music so deeply for so long that he forgot the taste of meat. *Shao* music was the music popular in Yu and Shun Era, a prosperous era in ancient China. Confucius lauded its "beauty and perfection to the extremity", and said, "*Shao* music, the musical heritage from Shun Era, is so touching and beautiful." People of Qi were all impressed by Confucius' love for music.

孔子与友人相聚时，听到友人唱出一首好歌，便　　并为学习到一首好歌而感到无比快乐。
会热情地请友人再唱一遍，自己也会随着友人唱和，

◎孔子与友人和歌图
Singing songs with friends

◎孔庙大成殿
孔庙又称文庙，是供奉和祭祀
孔子的地方。大成殿是孔庙的正殿。

Whenever his friends sang a good song, Confucius would ask them to sing again so that he could sing along. Confucius derived great joys from learning new songs.

齐景公接见孔子，并向孔子问政。孔子直言："为政在于节约财用。"事后学生问孔子为何如此回答，孔子说："齐景公奢侈地修盖楼榭、扩建花园，歌妓舞乐不停地表演，一个早晨就三次将拥有千辆战车的食邑封给臣下，所以我告诉他政在节财。"

◎孔子政在节财图
Practice frugality to administer a country

◎至圣林坊

至圣林即孔林，是孔子及其后裔墓地。孔林大门始建于元代至顺二年（1331年），大门牌坊为明代永乐二十二年（1424年）添建。

Duke Jing of Qi consulted Confucius about how to govern a country. Confucius shared without reservation: Practice frugality. His disciples all wondered. Confucius explained, "Duke Jing squandered a lot of money on palaces, gardens and entertainment. He even bestowed to his courtiers thousands of carriages three times on the same morning. Therefore, I told him to practice frugality."

蹴鞠，中国古代一种类似足球的体育活动。在春秋时期，蹴
鞠是训练士兵、考察兵将体格的方式。

　　孔子在齐国大臣高昭子的帮助下，见到了齐景公，听到了韶乐，也观看了当时临淄流行的"蹋鞠"（即蹴鞠），并被场上友人的高超球技所吸引。当时临淄重大庆典上都安排有蹴鞠比赛，孔子的齐国友人和学生中有很多人是蹴鞠爱好者。

孔子临淄观齐国友人蹴鞠时曾赴齐国临淄逗三年
观看了方将演行的蹴鞠鞠莘鞠场上
右人高超的球技研吸引孔子和文小
国友人和楼子生身而多人足《蹴鞠爱好者

◎孔子临淄观齐国友人蹴鞠图
Watching Cuju football

Confucius watched Cuju match, the earliest style of football in the world and was impressed by the players' sportsmanship. Cuju matches were organized for important celebration ceremonies. Many of Confucius disciples and friends in Qi were fans of Cuju football.

诸子百家国风画传

The Pictorial Biographies of Great Thinkers

孔子

图／文 郭德福

译 秦悦

画传 下册

CONFUCIUS Ⅱ

济南出版社

孔子画传
CONFUCIUS

目录
Contents
下册

齐景公通过与孔子多次深谈，想重用孔子，连送给孔子的封地都想好了，却遭到大臣们的反对，甚至到了有人想害死孔子的地步。情势紧急，孔子亟须离齐归鲁。孔子发现学生已经将米淘进炊具，尚未煮熟。为了避免浪费，他亲自动手将米捞出，接浙（捧着已经淘湿的米）而行。

◎孔子打包接淅图
Escaping for Lu

Duke Jing of Qi intended to appoint Confucius an important position. He even thought about conferring Confucius fiefdom. But his ministers were all strongly against it, and some of them even thought of murdering Confucius. Confucius had to leave Qi for Lu in a hurry. Seeing his disciples packing the cooking utensil with rice in, he scooped the rice out and walked with the rice in his palms.

孔子离齐归鲁途中路过泰山。为了一观泰山日出的壮美景象,他不畏山路险峻,勇攀泰山高峰。望着东方冉冉而起的朝阳,孔子心里充满仁者乐山的情怀。

On his way back to the State of Lu, Confucius climbed all the way up to the top of Mount Tai to admire the spectacular view of sunrise. Seeing the sun coming out from the east, Confucius' heart was filled with joy.

◎梁公林大门

　　梁公林，亦称启圣王林，位于曲阜城东，北靠327国道，南倚防山，北临泗水，是孔子的父亲叔梁纥、母亲颜征在的墓地。

生活中的孔子是个很重亲情的人。孔子同父异母的哥哥孟皮先天患有足疾，孔子多次回乡看望哥哥一家。兄弟俩灯窗夜话，手足情深。孔子教孟皮的儿子孔蔑识字读书，教诲他成长为德才兼备的人，还把自己的优秀学生南宫适介绍给孟皮的女儿为婿。孟皮去世后，孔子将哥哥葬在了防山父母墓旁。

Confucius valued family ties. Whenever Confucius went back home, he would visit his brother who was born with a lame leg, and they would talk into the depth of night. Confucius taught his brother's son Kong Mie to read and write, and told him to study hard to become a ethical and competent man. Confucius married his brother's daughter off to his disciple Nangong Shi. When his brother died, Confucius buried him by the side of his parents' tomb.

◎孔子还乡与孟皮夜话图
A reunion with brother

孔子诗礼传家图

史载孔子之子孔鲤早逝其孙子思即孙三代曾好学论语中孔子尝坦庭训教育孔鲤学诗学礼的特节流传千年中国家庭诗礼传家的文化渊源于此诗礼传家图谓诗礼传家之世

福德堂题

子曰："兴于诗，立于礼，成于乐。"（《论语·泰伯》）

　　孔子很重视对儿子孔鲤的文化教育，除让孔鲤与学生们一起听他讲学外，还关注他的学业选择与治学进程。《论语》记载，孔子曾两次教导孔鲤，说："不学诗，在社会交往中就不会说话；不学礼，在社会上做人做事，就不能立足。"孔子以诗礼传家的方式教育儿子孔鲤和孙子子思，使他们成为杰出的儒家学者。

◎孔子诗礼传家图

Confucius on poetry and rites

Confucius attached great importance to his son Kong Li's learning. Kong Li attended to his father's lecture and studied with his father's disciples. According to *The Analects of Confucius*, Confucius said, "If you do not learn something about poetry, your language will not be as elegant as powerful; if you do not learn something about rites, your conduct will not be proper in society." Confucius' teaching about poetry and rites entered into and colored his son Kong Li and grandson Zisi's consciousness. They are all distinguished scholars of Confucianism.

孔子基于人生不同阶段的生理状况，提出了"养生三戒"、"阶段养生"的理论。孔子说："君子有三戒：少之时，血气未定，戒之在色；及其壮也，血气方刚，戒之在斗；及其老也，血气既衰，戒之在得。" 强调在不同的时期，要遵循不同的养生规律。少年时，生理结构尚处于发育期，血气未定，过早沉湎色欲之中，会影响身体的正常发育与健康；壮年时期，血气方刚，身体发育完全，精力充沛，易怒好斗，因此应当"戒斗"；老年时，血气衰落，应该注意养生，忌贪心不足、欲望过多，应该"戒贪""戒得"。

Confucius proposed three abstentions in accordance with one's physical development. Confucius said, "a gentleman should refrain himself from sensuality when he is young and not fully developed, from competition and aggression when he is in his prime age and fully matured, from greed when he is old and physically declined."

◎ 孔子「养生三戒」图

Confucius on health preservation

子曰："君子喻于义，小人喻于利。"（《论语·里仁》）

　　鲁国的一位盲人乐师来见孔子，孔子亲自去迎接，扶他入席，并把在座的人谁坐在什么位置上一一介绍给他。乐师走后，学生子张问："老师，你今天这样对待盲人乐师，是不是以后我们遇见盲人，也应该这样做？"孔子回答："这本来就是帮助盲人最基本的方式呀。"

◎孔子助残图
Helping the blind

A blind musician of Lu paid a visit to Confucius. Confucius met him cordially and helped seat him. Confucius introduced those who were present to the musician. His disciple Zizhang asked Confucius, "Master, you received the blind musician in such a way, should we do the same thing when we meet the blind?" Confucius said, "That's what we are supposed to do."

在山东汶上，有孔子钓鱼台遗址。《论语》记载，"子钓而不纲"，意思是孔子不用多钩的网捕鱼，或者只用有一个鱼钩的钓竿垂钓。在利用自然资源的同时，保护自然资源循环往复、生生不息，孔子为现代人做出了榜样。

子曰："天何言哉？四时行焉，万物生焉。天何言哉？"
（《论语·阳货》）

According to *The Analects of Confucius,* Confucius went fishing using nets with a few hooks, or he simply used a fishing rod with a single hook. Fishing Terrace in Wenshang City in Shandong Province is the site where Confucius used to fish. Confucius set an example for modern people of utilizing natural resources without exhausting them.

◎孔子钓而不纲图
Confucius on fishing

孔子51岁时，被鲁定公任命为中都宰。孔子上任后，制定了一系列休养生息的惠民政策，仅一年，就使中都"路不拾遗，夜不闭户"，百姓安居乐业。孔子得到升迁，百姓前来送行。孔子婉言谢绝了百姓们送来的土特产品，独有一老人连夜为孔子赶做了一双布鞋，希望换孔子脚上的旧鞋为念。孔子很感动，亦理解老人换鞋的深意，欣然应允，留履中都。孔子穿着新鞋上路了，他感到了温暖，也感受到了百姓的心意。

◎孔子中都留履图
Bidding farewell to Zhongdu

Confucius was appointed mayor of Zhongdu city at 51. Confucius formulated a range of policies favoring the populace. Only one year after he took office, Zhongdu saw a peaceful and prosperous time. Things left behind by the sidewalk would never be taken, and unbolted doors would never be broken into at night. When Confucius got promoted, local people all saw him off and showered him with various gifts, but Confucius only took a pair of shoes. An elderly made the shoes specifically for Confucius to exchange for his old pair as a souvenir. Confucius was so moved that he left his old pair in Zhongdu. The new shoes, and the respect and love from common people urged Confucius to embark on his new journey.

孔子打假图

史载孔子任大司寇时，针对制假贩假之风，刑政相参，德法兼施。沈犹氏等不敢再以注水之羊高价收敛贩假行为。余特绘斯图以记之。乙未冬 荆趾 郭德福道

孔子升任鲁国大司寇，主管治安、司法。当时的曲阜制假贩假成风，有个叫沈犹氏的羊贩子就是这样的奸商。他大清早给羊灌喝大量的水，然后售卖，常年如此。还有些家畜贩子更是以次充好，不择手段抬高售价，欺骗民众。孔子上任后决心打假。他"刑政相参"，德法结合，经过认真治理，取得了显著的效果。奸商们收敛了贩假行为，沈犹氏再也不敢卖注水的羊了，家畜贩子也不敢以次充好乱涨价了。一些违法乱纪、制假贩假，又不思悔改的人，因害怕打击而逃出鲁国，整个社会和谐一新。

◎孔子打假图
Cracking down on counterfeit

Confucius was promoted the Minister of Law, in charge of public security and justice. Faking was rife in Qufu at that time. A dealer sold water-instilled mutton, some dealers sold lame livestock for high prices. Confucius took measures to both crack down the fraud and educate the local people, and the entire society took on a new look.

子曰："奢则不孙，俭则固。与其不孙也，宁固。"（《论语·述而》）

　　孔子升任鲁国大司寇后，位高权重，却谢辞了国君分配给他的好车骏马。孔子不讲排场，不比阔气，出行"乘柴车而驾驽马"（柴车指简朴的木马车，驽马意为跑不快的普通劣马）。孔子以身作则，倡导节俭，使鲁国奢侈之风有所改变，也给为官者做出了表率。

◎孔子柴车驽马倡俭图

A frugal Confucius

As a Minister of Law, Confucius was entitled to coach and steed, but he declined. His lifestyle was free from ostentation, and he traveled with simple coach and ordinary horses. Confucius set an example for other officials to practice frugality.

公元前500年夏，齐、鲁两国在夹谷（今山东莱芜境内）会盟。会盟时，齐国以表演为名，派人舞刀动戈，企图劫持鲁国国君。危急时刻，身为鲁国大司寇的孔子奋不顾身，直面刀戈，大声斥责齐人失礼，以正义战胜齐国，使鲁国取得了夹谷会盟的胜利。孔子以礼做武器，维护了国家的尊严和利益。

见利思义，见危授命，久要不忘平生之言，亦可以为成人矣。（《论语·宪问》）

In 500 BC, the Dukes of Qi and Lu met in a valley to discuss the possible alliance. However, Qi intended to kidnap the Duke of Lu in a sword-holding performance they presented. Confucius stood out in this crisis, denouncing Qi for showing no respect to rites. His righteousness in practicing rites not only frightened off Qi, but also safeguarded the dignity of the Duke and the interests of Lu.

◎孔子夹谷会盟正义护国图
Practicing rites to safeguard the interests of Lu

三桓，指鲁国卿大夫季孙氏、叔孙氏、孟孙氏。由于三家皆为鲁桓公之后代，故人们称之为"三桓"。

孔子任大司寇代摄相事时，为了实现国家安定统一，提出了"堕三都"的建议，主张把季孙氏、叔孙氏、孟孙氏的费、郈、成三邑城墙拆除，从而削弱"三桓"的势力。在实施中，费邑的公山不狃率军反叛，偷袭国都，孔子率曲阜军民合力击败叛军。孔子在拆除成邑城墙时又遭到孟孙氏的强烈反对，"堕三都"计划失败。"三桓"对孔子的不满与疑虑加重，孔子在鲁国政坛陷入困境。

◎孔子"堕三都"图
Demolishing the city walls

To unify and stabilize the State, Confucius proposed to undermine the three powerful clans by leveling the walls surrounding the city in their fiefdom. However, his proposal met with a strong resistance. One powerful clan rebelled and attacked the capital city though was defeated by the army Confucius commanded. Another clan also opposed strongly. Confucius' plan to weaken their power fell through. The displeasure and distrust the three clans held against Confucius trapped him in a very difficult political situation.

子曰："德不孤，必有邻。"（《论语·里仁》）

　　孔子辅政使鲁国日益强大，齐国君臣感到了威胁，他们想出一计，送给鲁定公许多美女、良马，使鲁定公、季桓子"往观终日，怠于政事"。鲁国郊祭大典后，季氏未按常规分送祭肉给孔子，这意味着孔子被鲁国政坛抛弃了。孔子师生决定离开鲁国，去别国另寻出路。孔子一行在屯地遇到季桓子派来送行的师己，孔子见他只是送行并非挽留，很是失望。临行之际，他说："迟迟吾行也，去父母国之道也。"表达了他对鲁国的留恋与热爱。就这样，已经55岁的孔子离开鲁国，开始了漫长的周游列国生涯。

◎孔子离鲁图
Leaving Lu for other countries

Confucius helped to make Lu a rising power so that the neighboring state Qi felt threatened. They contrived a plan to sow discord. Qi presented Duke Ding of Lu and his ministers beautiful ladies and handsome horses,so they started to indulge in pleasure−seeking. Confucius fell into disfavor and decided to seek development elsewhere. The 55−year old Confucius left Lu reluctantly and started traveling across different countries.

据说舜继部落联盟首领之位时，带领百姓祭拜天地，吟咏《南风》，后人将这一天作为岁首，这就是春节的由来。《南风》表达了养民爱物的和谐气象，为历代所推崇。孔子喜爱弦歌此诗，他评价说："德如泉流，至于今，王公大人述而弗忘。"孔子师生按家乡习俗垒起枣馒头山，演奏《南风》，守岁过春节。

◎孔子师生弦歌《南风》迎新图
Singing *Nanfeng* to celebrate the Spring Festival

Legend has it that when Shun succeeded to throne, he led his people to worship the heaven and earth, reciting *Nanfeng*, and thus this day was regarded as the beginning of a year, and also the origin of the Spring Festival. *Nanfeng* depicts a harmonious picture of people and nature. Confucius played this lyric poem to celebrate the Spring Festival.

◎孔子倡导诚信图
Confucius on credit

信近于义，言可复也。（《论语·学而》）

孔子只在卫国居住了10个月就被迫离开，打算去晋国。途中，孔子对学生说："人而无信，不知其可也。大车无輗，小车无軏，其何以行之哉！"孔子认为人没有诚信，就像牛拉的大车和马拉的小车缺少套牲口的活销一样，怎么能走呢？

Confucius only stayed in Wei for about ten months and was forced to leave for the State of Jin. He made an analogy about one's credit on this trip, "If a man loses his credit, how could he conduct himself in the world? Just like a cart or a carriage, what's its use without yoke?"

　　孔子带着学生周游列国，栉风沐雨，传道授业，寻找实现理想的机会。一次，孔子师生在赶往宋国的途中，于一棵大树下燃起篝火，开始讲学。宋国司马桓魋因听说孔子批评他造石椁三年未完工，浪费了人力物力，而怀恨在心，派人前来砍倒大树，扬言要加害孔子。孔子师生只得连夜赶往郑国。

◎孔子周游列国途中讲学图
Lecturing under a tree

Confucius continued his lecture tour, hoping he could be entrusted to administering a state. However, Confucius could never stay in a state for long before he was empowered. He criticized a minister of Song for wasting three years' time and a huge amount of money on building a stone coffin. The minister sent his people to cut down the tree under which Confucius gave lectures. Confucius and his disciples had to leave for the State of Zheng overnight.

孔子师生在去郑国的路上走散了，孔子一人站在东城门口，样子惶恐落魄。子贡焦急地到处寻找老师，这时一个路人告诉他："东城门站着一人，落魄得像一只丧家狗。"子贡寻到孔子并将此话告诉了老师，孔子听后没有生气，欣然受之且赞叹道："然哉（说得真像啊）！然哉！"

Confucius got thoroughly lost on his way to Zheng. He stood at the gate, looking despondent. Zigong looked about for him. A passerby told the anxious disciple, "There is an old man standing at the eastern entrance of the city, as despondent as a lost dog." When Confucius was told so, he was too ready to agree.

◎孔子然哉图
Getting lost

子曰："岁寒，然后知松柏之后凋也。"（《论语·子罕》）

公元前489年，孔子带领学生前往楚国。陈、蔡两国国君担心孔子去楚国后会对他们不利，于是派人将孔子师生围困在陈、蔡之间的孤岛上。孔子师生断粮七日，学生饿的饿，病的病。孔子却十分镇定安详，依然给学生们讲课、诵诗、弹琴，没有停止。七日后，孔子一行人终于脱离困境。

◎孔子弦歌图
Playing the music calmly in a desperate plight

Confucius left for the State of Chu in 489 BC. However, the Dukes of Chen and Cai worried that Confucius would be a threat to them. They kept Confucius and his disciples on an island between Chen and Cai. Confucius and his disciples had nothing to eat and drink for seven days, and some of them were starved to illness. But Confucius was not affected by the short supply at all. He stayed calm and continued his lecture and music as usual. They were finally saved seven days later.

孔子在从卫适曹、去陈赴楚的周游奔波中，虽没实现最终的政治抱负，却在磨难和挫折中养成了高尚的品格，丰富了学养，完美了德行。在旅途小憩的篝火旁，在粟米粥的香气里，奔波劳累的孔子渐入梦乡——象征着祥和盛世的金凤凰展翅飞来，清明仁政得以实施，"有教无类"惠及天下学子，"路不拾遗，夜不闭户"的和谐景象呈现乡里……

Confucius traveled from country to country with his thwarted ambition. He enriched his knowledge and cultivated his morality in exile. In his weary sleep, he dreamed of realizing his political aspirations: a peaceful and prosperous era with phoenix flying above, people getting the education they want, fair and just governing of a state …

◎孔子之梦图
The dream of Confucius

子曰："志于道，据于德，依于仁，游于艺。"（《论语·述而》）

孔子在周游列国途中，得知齐国大军要进犯鲁国，鲁国危在旦夕。孔子急派学生子贡去游说诸侯国，为鲁国抗齐争取准备时间。孔子又送简函给已归鲁的学生冉求、樊迟，两位学生遂按照孔子教授的"射""御"之术训练了一支手执长戈的突击队。冉求挂帅，率鲁军以长戈力克齐军的刀剑，大败齐军，遂解鲁国之危。大胜之后，有人问冉求率军胜齐的本领是从何处学来的，冉求答是从老师孔子那里学来的。

A troop of Qi invaded Lu, and Lu was at risk. Confucius sent his disciple Zigong to lobby other states to remain neutral so that Lu could get ready for the war. Meanwhile, he wrote to Ran Qiu and Fan Chi, who had been back in Lu, to train the army to defend. Ran Qiu and Fan Chi defeated the invasion. When asked who their master was, Ran Qiu said it was Confucius who taught them all.

孔子师生救鲁图
Saving Lu from war

子曰："三军可夺帅也，匹夫不可夺志也。"（《论语·子罕》）

　　孔子的学生冉求、樊迟在鲁国危难之时敢于担当，分率左右两军抗击入侵强敌。当鲁军面临险境时，樊迟大声鼓励士兵为保卫国家而战，并身先士卒，第一个杀入敌军；冉求则挥长戈力战克敌，大败齐军。孔子知道后，欣慰地说："真是义士啊。"

◎孔子学生冉求、樊迟报国图
Ran Qiu and Fan Chi fighting for their country

Confucius' disciples Ran Qiu and Fan Chi rose to the challenge when Lu was in danger. They each led an army and forced their way into the enemy. Fan Chi encouraged his soldiers to fight and was always the one to charge ahead. Ran Qiu brandished his broadsword to fight. When Confucius learned that, he said with relief and pride, "What brave men they are!"

◎ 孔子爱兰图
An orchid on the rocks

且芝兰生于深林，不以无人而不芳；君子修道立德，不谓穷困而改节。（《孔子家语·在厄》）

公元前 484 年，季康子派人迎孔子回鲁国，时年 68 岁的孔子终于结束了 14 年颠沛流离的生活，返回故乡。途经隐谷，孔子看到长在乱草中的兰花，它的高雅，它的馨美，都令孔子流连。他便抚琴作歌《猗兰操》，

歌道："山风习习吹着，天阴要下雨了。他要回归远方，送他到野外。为什么苍天之下没有他的处所，辽阔的九州没有他安定的居处？世人不认识贤能的人。岁月流逝，我将衰老了。"

Ji Kangzi requested earnestly that Confucius come back to Lu in 484 B.C. The 68-year old Confucius finally came back home after a 14-year exile. The orchid blooming on the rock inspired Confucius to play and sing a song expressing his mixed feelings of coming home， "Why there is no home for him, why there is no one recognizing his talent? Time passes swiftly, I'm getting old quickly ."

◎孔子编《春秋》图
Working on *The Spring and Autumn Annals*

　　返回鲁国后，孔子潜心向学。曲阜息陬村是孔子修订《春秋》、整理古籍的地方，此村因孔子在此作《息陬操》而闻名。《春秋》是我国第一部编年体史书，记载了春秋时期242年的历史，内容涉及当时的政治、军事、经济、文化、天文气象、物质生产、社会生活等诸方面。《春秋》本是孔子给学生编纂的历史课本，特创了编年体史书笔法，隐寓褒贬，婉而成章。《春秋》不但收录档案，还加入了孔子的看法，孔子曾叹曰："知我者，其惟《春秋》乎！罪我者，其惟《春秋》乎！"

◎洙泗书院

洙泗书院是孔子周游列国返回鲁国后整理文献、从事教育的地方。

When in Lu, Confucius was finally able to settle down on study. Confucius edited *The Spring and Autumn Annals*. *The Spring and Autumn* Annals is the first annals in Chinese history, recording a 242-year history during the Spring and Autumn Period. The annals cover political, military, economic, cultural, meteorological and social aspects. *The Spring and Autumn Annals* is actually a history book Confucius complied for students. The book is a valuable collection of document with Confucius annotations. For the compilation of *The Spring and Autumn Annals*, Confucius said, "There are people who will appreciate what I have done, but there are also people who will criticize me. Ultimately history will have the final say."

子夏是孔子门下文学科的青年才俊，他一直帮助晚年的孔子进行文化典籍整理，为孔子的得力助手。孔子将《诗经》中的诗全部谱曲后，传授给子夏。当时孔子倡导诗与乐不能分开，诗可吟可唱。他用配乐之诗叙事言志，在弦歌吟唱中交流沟通，让诗、乐、礼成为一体，成就了"兴于诗，立于礼，成于乐"的孔门教育体系。

◎孔子传乐子夏图
A promising disciple to succeed Confucius

Zixia was a promising young disciple of Confucius, and he assisted the elderly Confucius to classify archives. Confucius compiled the scores he composed for all poems in *The Book of Songs* and taught them to Zixia. Confucius advocated that poetry and music were inseparable, and poems could sing well in songs. That "thriving on poetry, standing on formality, succeeding on music" is Confucius' teaching philosophy.

在爷爷孔子的关爱下，子思一天天长大。当他能背出书中的简单诗句时，孔子欣慰地笑了。子思不负爷爷的教诲，后来经过一番努力，成为著名的儒家学者。孟子便是子思的学生，四书五经中的《中庸》也出自子思的手笔。

◎孔子听子思背诗图
Zisi reciting poems

Confucius had the joy of seeing Zisi growing up. Confucius smiled with such a pride when Zisi could recite poems. Zisi didn't fall short of his expectation. He studied hard and made himself a great scholar. He was the teacher of Mencius and the author of *The Golden Mean*.

◎先师手植桧

相传此桧树是孔子亲手种植，位于山东曲阜孔庙内。

孔子爱植树，多次和学生在杏坛前种树，有一株当年孔子亲手植下的桧树，至今仍枝繁叶茂。孔子去看望女婿公冶长一家时，带去的礼物就是几株树苗。孔子与学生在河南上蔡县种下的一棵银杏树，至今仍生机勃勃。

◎孔子师生植树图
Planting trees

Confucius liked planting trees. He planted trees with his disciples on many occasions. When Confucius visited his son-in-law, the gifts he brought with him were also some seedling. One tree he planted in Shangcai survives till today with luxurious leaves.

一次叶公问孔子的学生子路："你的老师是个什么样的人？"子路没有回答。子路回去后将此事告诉了孔子。孔子说："你何不告诉他，我发愤研求学问，常常忘了吃饭；当学问有所发现与长进，就会快乐得忘了忧愁，甚至忽略了衰老的到来。"孔子的忘忧是真正的快乐，这种终生好学、物我两忘的真快乐，是人生的最高境界。

子曰："女奚不曰：其为人也，发愤忘食，乐以忘忧，不知老之将至云尔。"（《论语·述而》）

Zilu was once asked, "What do you think of your master?" Zilu didn't answer. Zilu went back and told Confucius the question. Confucius said, "You could tell him that I will forget to eat when I immerse myself in study, I'll forget unhappiness and even aging when I make some progress in study." Learning made Confucius forget both himself and the external world, bringing him inner peace and joy.

◎孔子乐而忘忧图
A contented learner

孔子家养过一只犬，孔子很爱此犬，常常带它散步。他在杏坛讲学时，此犬静卧一旁似在听课，并养成了"爱简书"的习惯。孔子师生在院中晾晒的简书，它从不践踏，总会绕"书"而行。有一天，此犬老死了，孔子很伤心，对学生子贡说："把它好好安葬吧，我听说马死了是用旧的车帷幕包起来埋葬的，犬死后是用旧的车盖盖着埋葬的。我穷，没有旧车盖，你就拿领席子把它包起来埋掉吧。"于是，子贡带人将此犬埋在了孔子常带它散步的泗水边。

◎孔子爱犬图
Confucius and his dog

Confucius once kept a dog. The dog went walk with him, sat in his class, and gradually developed a love for books. He never set his foot on the books Confucius and his disciples laid bare under the sun. The dog died of aging. Confucius said sadly to his disciple Zigong, "Bury him in a decent way. I was told that a horse is buried with old curtain of the coach he drawn, and a dog is buried with a roof the coach. I'm very poor and I don't have a coach. So just bury him with a mattress." Zigong buried him on the bank of Sishui River where Confucius always took the dog for a walk.

孔子71岁时，他心爱的学生，年仅41岁的颜回去世。白发孔子放声痛哭："哎呀！老天要我的命啊！老天要我的命啊！"学生们怕老师伤了身体，围过来劝他，孔子又哭道："我不为这样的人伤心，还为什么人伤心呢？"孔子是在为一位理想的接班人早逝而哭泣，折射出了一位老师对学生金子般的爱心。孔子与颜回情同父子的师生情谊，也成为中国传统文化中的经典故事流传下来。

When Confucius was 71, his favorite student Yan Hui died at an early age of 41. Confucius wailed for his premature death. His disciples asked him to restrain his grief, but Confucius said, "If I don't cry for such a good person, who else should I feel grief over for?" Confucius felt so grief-stricken, because Yan Hui would be the ideal successor to him.

◎孔子哭颜回图
Wailing over Yan Hui's death

◎颜庙

颜庙即复圣庙，位于曲阜陋巷街北首，是祭祀颜回的庙宇。

◎孔子墓

位于山东省曲阜市孔林中偏南地段，是孔林的中心所在。孔子墓初以砖砌祠坛，唐易以泰山封禅石，元、明先后刻立墓碑。

公元前479年4月11日，73岁的孔子与世长辞。孔子临终前唱道："泰山其颓乎！梁木其坏乎！哲人其萎乎！（泰山崩了！天柱折了！哲人去了！）"孔子去世后被葬在曲阜城北泗水岸边。学生们为纪念孔子，将他的言论汇编成《论语》一书，成为经典文献。司马迁在《史记·孔子世家》中这样评价孔子："高山仰止，景行行止（像高山一样让人瞻仰，像大道一样让人遵循）。"孔子在他漫长的教育生涯中，教育出三千学子，是开创我国平民教育的第一人。这位伟大的教育家、思想家，他的思想学说影响了世界两千多年，并将不断延续下去。

◎孔子高山仰止图
A great thinker

On April 11, 479 BC, Confucius died at age 73. His last words were "Mount Tai collapsing, the pillar breaking and the saint dying". To commemorate his achievements, his disciples compiled his lectures into *The Analects of Confucius*. As a great educator and thinker, Confucius taught more than three thousand elite students in his long and fruitful education career, and his philosophy is still influencing the world.

孔门十哲 （孔子门下最优秀的十位学生）
Ten great disciples of Confucius

闵损，字子骞，比孔子小十五岁，鲁国人。闵损以德行著称，孔子特别表彰他的孝行，说他顺事父母，友爱兄弟。闵损幼年时遭后母虐待，他的父亲知道以后，非常愤怒，要把后妻赶走，闵损反而为后母求情。他说，母在一子寒，母去三子单。因为后母生了两个孩子，如果后母被赶走了，那三个孩子就没人照顾了。他的孝行感动了父母，也深得远近之人的赞赏。他被列为孔门四科十哲（德行科）之一。

Min Sun, honorary title Ziqian. Min Sun was from the State of Lu and was 15 years younger than Confucius. Confucius praised him for his filial piety for his parents and his love for his brothers. Min Sun's step-mother treated him very badly when he was very young. His father was very furious and asked his step-mother to pack away. Min Sun pleaded that though his step-mother did not treat him well, at least his two other half-brothers had their own mother around to take care of them. Min Sun's forgiveness moved his parents and their neighbors.

颜回，字子渊，亦称颜渊，比孔子小三十岁，鲁国人。颜回出身贫贱，一生没有做官。孔子称赞他说：「颜回真是难得啊！用一个竹筒吃饭，用一个瓜瓢喝水，住在陋巷里。要是一般人，一定忧烦难受，可颜回却安然处之，没有改变向道好学的乐趣。」颜回敏而好学，能闻一知十，注重仁德修养，深得孔子欣赏和喜爱。他被列为孔门四科十哲（德行科）之一。

Yan Hui, honorary title Ziyuan, also known as Yan Yuan. Yan Hui was born into a humble family in the State of Lu and was 30 years younger than Confucius. Yan Hui never took any official post in his life. Confucius praised him for his attitude toward life and pursuit of aspiration: "How worthy Yan Hui is! He lives in a shabby place, eats with bamboo container, and drinks from a gourd. Other people will find this life unendurable, but Yan Hui can take it all and enjoy learning in such environment." Yan Hui was both bright and studious, and was of the Confucius favorite students.

【冉雍】Ran Yong

孔门四科十哲（德行科）之一。可以做地方长官。他被列为认为冉雍具有君子的容度，默厚重，深得孔子的器重，也不好。冉雍气量宽宏，沉来；父亲不好，儿子不一定口。孔子驳斥说，一头耕牛，有人以此作为攻击冉雍的借身贫贱，他的父亲行为不良，二十九岁，鲁国人。冉雍出冉雍，字仲弓，比孔子小也可以生出献祭用的小牛

Ran Yong, honorary title Zhonggong. Ran Yong was from the State of Lu and was 29 years younger than Confucius. Ran Yong was born into a poor family and was often humiliated because of his father's bad conduct. Ran Yong was very forgiving and Confucius thought he had the tolerance and bearing to be a high-ranking official.

【冉耕】Ran Geng

科）之一。被列为孔门四科十哲（德行竟然会染上这种恶病！』他这也是天命啊！这样的好人，着说：『如果没有希望的话，站在窗外握着他的手，叹息人。孔子去探望他的时候，冉耕患了麻风病，不愿意见鲁国人，以德行著称。后来，冉耕，字伯牛，比孔子小七岁，

Ran Geng, honorary title Boniu. Ran Geng was from the State of Lu and was 7 years younger than Confucius. Ran Geng was well-known for his moral integrity. Ran Geng suffered from leprosy and had to keep to himself. Confucius went to visit him, and sighed, "It's so unfair that such disease preyed on such a good person."

诸子百家国风画传 177

端木赐，字子贡，比孔子小三十一岁，卫国人。他口才很好，雄辩滔滔，又能料事。曾担任鲁国和卫国之相，善于搞外交活动，曾在齐、吴、越、晋诸国间游说，使吴国攻齐，从而保全了鲁国。子贡与子路一文一武，犹如孔子的左右手。子贡善于经商，家境非常富有，是春秋时期著名的富商。孔子死后，子贡守墓六年，师生之情胜过父子。他被列为孔门四科十哲（言语科）之一。

Duanmu Ci, honorary title Zigong. Zigong was from the State of Wei and was 31 years younger than Confucius. Zigong was very eloquent and strong in diplomatic affairs. When he was the prime minister of Lu, he successfully negotiated between states and saved Lu from a war. Zigong had been a caretaker of Confucius' tomb for six years. The affection between teacher and student is stronger than that of father and son.

冉求，字子有，通称冉有，亦称有子，比孔子小二十九岁，鲁国人。冉求多才多艺，为孔子所称赞。冉求长于政事，尤其善于理财，曾任季氏宰。他能带兵作战。公元前484年任鲁国左师统帅，以步兵执长矛的战术打败了齐国。趁这次得胜的机会，他说服季康子迎回了在外流亡十四年的孔子。后来，由于冉求帮季康子聚敛民财，受到孔子严厉批评，但这并未影响他们师生间的关系，足见师生相知深厚。他被列为孔门四科十哲（政事科）之一。

Ran Qiu, honorary title Ziyou, also known as Youzi. Ran Qiu was from the State of Lu and was 29 years younger than Confucius. Ran Qiu was very versatile. He could both handle financial matters and command a troop. He defeated Qi and asked Ji Kangzi to invite Confucius back from his exile. Confucius criticized Ran Qiu for amassing wealth for Ji Kangzi, but that did not affect their teacher−student relationship at all.

【宰予】Zai Yu

宰予，字子我，也称宰我，鲁国人。宰予口齿伶俐，能说善辩，孔子常派遣他出使别国，如齐国、楚国等。宰予遇事有自己的主见，常与孔子讨论问题，并有独到的见解。他曾提出改『三年之丧』为『一年之丧』，即缩短丧期，遭到孔子的指责。宰予任齐国临淄大夫，因参与陈恒弑君事件而被杀。他被列为孔门四科十哲（言语科）之一。

Zai Yu, honorary title Ziwo, also known as Zaiwo. Zai Yu was eloquent, and Confucius always sent him as an envoy to many states. He dared to voice his opinion on whatever matters he discussed with Confucius. He suggested that the mourning period for one's parent should be shortened from three years to one year, but Confucius criticized him harshly. Zai Yu was killed for his involvement in an assassination.

【仲由】Zhong You

仲由，字子路，因他曾为季氏的家臣，又被称作季路，比孔子小九岁，鲁国人。仲由出身微贱，家境贫寒，却生性豪爽，为人耿直，有勇力才艺。仲由经常批评孔子，孔子也常批评他，仲由闻过则喜，能虚心接受。孔子对他评价很高。仲由做过鲁国的季氏宰，做过卫国大夫孔悝的邑宰。他被列为孔门四科十哲（政事科）之一。

Zhong You, honorary title Zilu. Zhong You was born into a poor family in the State of Lu, and was 9 years younger than Confucius. Zhong You was very upright and straightforward. He often criticized Confucius and Confucius criticized him, too. But Zhong You was glad to have his errors pointed out, and Confucius thought highly of him for that.

郭德福冒雨寻访孔子观礼处
Guo Defu visiting where
Confucius reviewing the
ceremony

郭德福在汶上县了解孔子中都留履的典故
Guo Defu in Wenshang County learning
more about Confucius' leaving a pair of
shoes when bidding farewell to Zhongdu

郭德福在尼山孔子出生地夫子洞前，
许下完成孔子画传的心愿

Guo Defu making his wish to paint
Confucius' life in front of the cave where
Confucius was born

[Author's Notes] Why I want to paint Confucius

In 1988, 75 Nobel Prize winners gathered in Paris for a joint statement, appealing to the whole world to learn from Confucius' wisdom in order to survive in the 21st century. The 21st century has witnessed much social unrest worldwide, and that made me hard to confine myself in my studio. Since 2004, I went to Shandong Province and Henan Province many times, following Confucius footsteps. I visited his residence and interviewed his descendents. I paid numerous visits to the historical sites: his mother's tomb, the place he played music calmly when he and his disciples were in a life-and-death crisis, Yishui River where his disciples expressed their ambitions. Confucius is getting so close to me as if he were standing in front of me and smiling at me. I remember I was caught in a sudden storm when I went to the place where Confucius consulted Lao-tse. I was soaked all through, walking helplessly on the muddy country road. In a flash of lightning, I seemed to see Confucius sitting in a cart, plodding in the rain. I was moved to tears at what I visualized. I think I suddenly understood Confucius as a pioneer advocating "teaching without discrimination", and I also understood his trying to instill his philosophy of Benevolence into the rulers in order to realize his ideal. I was thus determined to paint Confucius' life in my lifetime in order to let more people understand what Confucius advocated more than 2500 years ago. His philosophies about being a man, a master, an official, a husband and about our relationship with Nature still remain insightful today.

If what I have painted about Confucius in recent 10 years can inspire readers' passion for Confucius cultural heritage, I can realize a dream I have cherished since my childhood—"serving my country with my painting".

My many thanks go to Xinhua News Agency for their 25 reports about my creation of Confucius series; my thanks also go to CCTV (China Central TV), *Guangming Daily, Beijing Youth Newspaper, Dazhong Daily, Shenyang Daily,* and *Lianhe Zaobao* (Singapore) and other European and American media for their coverage.

My gratitude goes to Mr. Liu Yajun of Shanghai Comic Book Center for his flight to Shenyang, and for browsing my creation of Confucius series in my studio and deciding to get it published; to Jinan Publishing House for publishing this book in Confucius' hometown. Finally, I want to thank all the people whose hard work made this publication possible.

Guo Defu
September 23, 2013

后记

中国国家主席习近平在谈及中华文化时，深刻地指出：

『中华优秀传统文化已经成为中华民族的基因，植根在中国人内心，潜移默化影响着中国人的思想方式和行为方式。』厚重、灿烂的中华传统文化，如何借由一种生动、直观、亲切的方式走进读者，尤其是海外读者的阅读视野中，一直是文化界关注、思索的问题。当《诸子百家国风画传》丛书带着『传承、创新、中国风』的鲜明印迹从上海出发，正是希望由此探索向世界传播、普及中国优秀传统文化的新方式和新渠道。

上海，作为国际文化大都市，通过源源不断地推出文化交流精品，成为海外读者了解中国、感受中国的一扇精彩窗口。发源于上海的连环画艺术，则以其浓郁、独特的中国韵味深受国内外读者的欢迎。两年前，以传承、振兴中国连环画艺术为主旨的上海海派连环画中心甫一成立，即在上海市政府新闻办的指导、创意下，联合发起策划一套以国风连环画为载体、契合『读图时代』特点的《诸子百家国风画传》丛书，并得到了国务院新闻办公室、中共上海市委宣传部的大力支持，以及山东、河南省政府新闻办和相关诸子故里的密切协作。

尤为可贵的是，国内著名国画家郭德福、李维定、赵明钧、邵家声、钱定华为淋漓再现智者先贤而实地采风、遍览典籍、泼墨挥毫，追寻中国文化符号世界化表达的崭新方式。画家们数易其稿，精益求精，创作出让人耳目一新、形神兼备的诸子形象。画传不仅选取诸子生平中最具典型意义的事件，还注意表现鲜有人关注的诸子日常生活。画传想让读者感知的不只是存在于文献、传说里的古之圣贤，更是身边熟悉亲切、可以答疑解惑的智者。

我们衷心希望，这套充满哲理智慧与中国艺术美质的丛书能够成为连接当代与中华传统的文化桥梁。希望中华文化的寻源之旅能让每一个中国人寻回精神归属，也让海外读者从另一蹊径了解中国文化之美。

《诸子百家国风画传》丛书编委会

二〇一四年九月

Afterword

President Xi Jinping made an insightful comment in his talking about Chinese culture, "The excellent traditional Chinese culture has become our genes deeply rooted in our heart, entered into and colored our patterns in thinking and behaving." How the rich and brilliant Chinese culture could be presented in a vivid, visual and approachable form to the readers, especially overseas readers, has always been the concern of the cultural circle. When *The Pictorial Biographies of Great Thinkers* series with its distinguishing features of "inheritance, originality, and Chinese style" is setting sail from Shanghai, it is hoped to be a new means and a new channel explored for spreading, popularizing the excellent Chinese culture.

As an international cultural metropolis, Shanghai has created continuously first-class cultural exchange project and has become a window through which overseas readers get to know and understand China. The comic book painting art originated in Shanghai has always been well accepted by readers home and abroad for its rich and unique Chinese style. Two years ago, not long after Shanghai Comic Book Center established to inherit and revive the comic painting art, under the guidance of Information Office of Shanghai Municipality, the Center created a series of comic book — *The Pictorial Biographies of Great Thinkers* to appeal to the "visual era". This innovative project is supported by Information Office of State Council and Publicity Ministry of Shanghai Municipal committee of CPC, and this project is also a close cooperation between Information Office of Shandong Provincial People's Government, Information Office of Henan Provincial People's Government and Confucius hometown.

What made this series particularly valuable is the research work the artists did. To represent thoroughly and faithfully the great thinkers, Mr. Guo Defu, Mr. Zhao Mingjun, Mr. Shao Jiasheng and Mr. Qian Dinghua, not only read extensively the classics but also conducted field work. They tried different means of expression and revised numerous times for a better unity of appearance and spirit of the thinkers. The episodes in the pictorial biographies reveal both the milestone events great thinkers experienced and their daily life that usually went unnoticed. The great thinkers in the pictorial biographies are no longer legendary figure in the literature, but amiable saints we can approach with our problems for a solution.

We sincerely hope that this series rich in philosophical wisdom and Chinese aestheticism could bridge the contemporary China and its traditional culture. We also hope that the exploration of Chinese culture will give every Chinese a sense of spiritual belonging, and provide an alternative for overseas readers to get to know the beauty of Chinese culture.

Editing Committee of *The Pictorial Biographies of Great Thinkers*
September 2014